World of Farming

Farm Machines

This item has been purchased with matching
funds from the Twinsburg Public Library and
the IMLS' State Library of Ohio
Growing Communities Grant.

Nancy Dickmann

Heinemann Library
Chicago, Illinois

www.heinemannraintree.com
Visit our website to find out
more information about
Heinemann-Raintree books.

To order:
☎ Phone 888-454-2279
💻 Visit www.heinemannraintree.com
to browse our catalog and order online.

©2011 Heinemann Library
an imprint of Capstone Global Library, LLC
Chicago, Illinois

Edited by Siân Smith, Nancy Dickmann, and Rebecca Rissman
Designed by Joanna Hinton-Malivoire
Picture research by Mica Brancic
Production by Victoria Fitzgerald
Originated by Capstone Global Library Ltd
Printed and bound in China by South China Printing Company Ltd

ISBN 978 1 4329 3928 1
15 14 13 12 11 10
10 9 8 7 6 5 4 3 2 1

Library of Congress Cataloging-in-Publication Data
Dickmann, Nancy.
  Farm machines / Nancy Dickmann. —1st ed.
      p. cm.—(World of farming)
  Includes bibliographical references and index.
  ISBN 978-1-4329-3928-1 (hc) —ISBN 978-1-4329-3942-7 (pb)
  1. Agricultural machinery—Juvenile literature. I. Title. II. Series: Dickmann,
Nancy. World of farming.
  S675.25.D53 2010
  631.3—dc22
                                          2009051567

Acknowledgements
We would like to thank the following for permission to reproduce
photographs: Photolibrary pp.**4** (Cultura/Bill Sykes), **5** (Britain on View/
Nature Picture Library), **6** (age fotostock/Javier Larrea), **7** (Design Pics
Inc.), **8** (Pixtal Images), **9** (Mark Pedlar), **10** (imagebroker.net/Guenter
Fischer), **11** (imagebroker.net/Markus Keller), **12** (Fresh Food Images/
Maximilian Stock Ltd), **14** (Creatas), **15** (All Canada Photos/Russ Heinl), **17**
(Pixtal Images), **18** (Oxford Scientific (OSF)/Martyn Chillmaid), **19** (Tips
Italia/Tommaso Di Girolamo), **22** (Pixtal Images), **23 top** (imagebroker.
net/Markus Keller), **23 middle top** (imagebroker.net/Guenter Fischer),
23 middle bottom (Pixtal Images), **23 bottom** (Fresh Food Images/
Maximilian Stock Ltd); Getty Images p.**21** (Warner Bros/Sergei Bachlakov);
iStockphoto p.**20** (© Susan H. Smith); Shutterstock pp.**13** (fotohunter), **16**
(Katharina Wittfeld).

Front cover photograph of a red tractor in a field reproduced with
permission of iStockPhoto (© Branko Miokovic). Back cover photograph of
a grape picking machine in Gironde, France reproduced with permission of
Photolibrary (Oxford Scientific (OSF)/Martyn Chillmaid).

The publisher would like to thank Dee Reid, Diana Bentley, and Nancy Harris
for their invaluable help with this book.

Every effort has been made to contact copyright holders of material
reproduced in this book. Any omissions will be rectified in subsequent
printings if notice is given to the publishers.

Contents

What Is a Farm?

A farm is a place where food is grown.

Farmers use many different machines.

Tractors

A tractor is a farm machine.

tractor

Tractors can pull other machines.

Planting

plow

A plow is a farm machine.

A plow digs up the ground so it is ready for planting.

A plow can be pulled by oxen.

manure

This farm machine spreads manure
to help plants grow.

Growing Plants

This machine plants seeds.

The seeds grow into plants.

water

This machine waters the plants.

insect spray

This machine kills harmful insects.

Picking Plants

These tomatoes are ready to pick.

wheat

This machine cuts wheat.

This machine picks grapes.

hay

This machine packs hay.

Taking Care of Farm Machines

Farm machines are very important.

Farmers must take good care of their machines.

Can You Remember?

What does a plow do?

Answer on page 24

Picture Glossary

 **manure** most manure is made from animal waste. It helps plants to grow.

 **oxen** cows or bulls that are trained to pull plows or do other farm jobs

 **plow** farm machine that breaks up the ground so that farmers can plant seeds

 **seed** plants grow from seeds. Farmers plant seeds in the ground.

Index

Answer to quiz on page 22: A plow digs up the ground to get it ready for planting.

Note to Parents and Teachers

Before reading:
Ask the children if they have ever visited a farm. Ask them what machines they might find on a farm. Make a list together and see if they know what each machine is used for. Why do they think farmers need machines?

After reading:
• Put the children into groups and give them a range of materials to make things with, such as cardboard boxes and tubes. Ask them to make a model of a tractor or other farm machine from the book. Make sure they have plenty of circular plastic or card to make wheels. When the models are ready, the children can paint them and make a farm display.

• Sing "This is the way we...," building in words about farm machines. For example: "This is the way we plow the field, plow the field, plow the field, This is the way we plow the field, Early in the morning." Other verses could start: "This is the way we pull the trailer," "This is the way we plant the seeds," "This is the way we cut the wheat," etc. You could hold up pictures of each machine to prompt the children once they have learned the song.